*Soliloquy on the
Earnest Money of the Soul*

MEDIAEVAL PHILOSOPHICAL TEXTS IN TRANSLATION
NO. 9

Marquette University Press
1131 West Wisconsin Avenue
Milwaukee 3, Wisconsin

ii

HUGH OF ST. VICTOR

# Soliloquy on the Earnest Money of the Soul

*Translated from the Latin*
*With an Introduction*

*By*

KEVIN HERBERT, Ph.D.
Classics Department, Bowdoin College, Maine

Marquette University Press
MILWAUKEE, WISCONSIN
1956

NIHIL OBSTAT:    Rev. John A. Schulien, S.T.D.,
                 Censor of Books, Milwaukee,
                 November 23, 1956

IMPRIMATUR:      ✠Most Rev. Albert G. Meyer, D.D.,
                 Archbishop of Milwaukee,
                 November 26, 1956

Library of Congress Catalogue Card No. 56-9141
PRINTED
IN
U. S. A.

iv

# *Preface*

The critical text used herein is that of K. Müller, "Hugo von St. Viktor: *Soliloquium de arrha animae* und *De vanitate mundi*," *Kleine Texte für Vorlesungen und Übungen*, ed. H. Leitzmann, No. 123 (Bonn 1913). I have also made considerable use of the notes to the text in Ledrus' French translation of the *Soliloquy*, the full title of which appears in the bibliography.

The completion of this study was materially helped by a generous grant from Indiana University, made while I was a member of the faculty of that institution. I also wish to express my thanks to the Rev. Gerard Smith, S.J., chairman of the Department of Philosophy in Marquette University and to the editors of *Mediaeval Texts in Translation* for their kind and helpful criticisms of one whose proper field is the classical languages and literatures.

A brief note on citations: short titles are used after the first complete citation of a modern work. Also, after each reference to a work of Hugh in the text, the reader is given the volume and column number in Migne's *Patrologiae Cursus, series Latina*, where the passage appears. The letters *PL* are used in reference to Migne's work.

Brunswick, Maine
November, 1955

# Introduction

## I. LIFE AND THOUGHT

Hugh of St. Victor, mediaeval philosopher, theologian, and mystic, was born in 1096 in the castle at Hartingham, Saxony, the eldest son of Conrad, Count of Blankenberg. He was educated in the monastery at Hamersleben and there took the habit of the Canons Regular of St. Augustine. About 1115 he went to the Abbey of St. Victor in Paris, the mother house of the community at Hamersleben. It was to this house that William of Champeaux had retired after being defeated by his pupil Abelard in the controversy over the problem of universals. When William was elected to the see of Chalons-sur-Marne in 1113 he was succeeded at the monastery by Gilduin, under whom Hugh was to spend the rest of his life in study, teaching, and writing. In 1125 Hugh took up teaching duties at the monastery, and from 1133 to his death in 1141 he was in charge of this work as director of the school. He has been styled *alter Augustinus,* not only because of doctrinal resemblances but also because his writings possess a similar charm and power to attract and enlighten those who read them.[1]

Hugh is recognized today as one of the most influential theologians, both dogmatic and mystical, of his time. He was also an advocate of the liberal arts, which he believed would aid in the study of theology, if rightly pursued within the hierarchy of the sciences. In fact, unlike St. Bernard and his own successors in the School of St. Victor he held that all knowledge was useful. Learn everything, he says; you will see afterwards that nothing is useless. (*Didascalion* 6, 3; *PL* 176, 801). This is an important principle in his view because in the ordered life of a monk a planned regimen of learning was a needful step toward the highest form of monastical activity, contemplation. Knowledge, like the habits of work and prayer, is to be acquired and developed in order to be transcended in a higher form of activity.[2] In his classification of the sciences he shows his Aristotelian side, but in his psychology he is distinctly Augustinian.[3] For him consciousness and introspection give evidence not only of the

---

[1] For a complete and excellent treatment of Hugh and his work see F. Vernet, *Dictionnaire de théologie catholique* VII (Paris, 1927) 240-308.
[2] See E. Gilson, *History of Christian Philosophy in the Middle Ages* (New York, 1955) 170.
[3] H. Ostler, "Die Psychologie des Hugo von St. Viktor," *Beiträge zur Geschichte der Philosophie des Mittelalters* VI, 1 (Münster i. W. 1906) is the basic study; see F. Copleston, S.J., *A History of Philosophy* II (London, 1950) 175-176, for a brief discussion.

existence of the soul but also of its spirituality and immateriality. (*Didascalion* 7, 17; *PL* 176, 825). The soul on the one hand being rational has personality of and through itself; the body on the other forms an element in human personality only because of its union with the rational spirit. (*De sacramentis* 2, 1, 11; *PL* 176, 409). In natural theology his contributions to its systematic advance include *a posteriori* arguments based on internal and external experience.[4] The primary proof rests upon the experienced fact of self-consciousness, a state which did not always maintain and which therefore is evidence that there was a time when the soul did not exist. Since it is not self-caused, it owes its existence to a necessary and self-existent being, God. (*De sacramentis* 1, 3, 10; *PL* 176, 219). The second proof is from the external, experienced fact of change, a process which requires a Cause, and the last proof is teleological in its approach, for it views the ordered harmony of the cosmos, which observance postulates a governing Providence. If by these arguments Hugh holds to the possibility of a natural knowledge of the existence of God, he is equally insistent on the necessity of faith, especially in the light of the weakened condition of man's faculties because of sin. Yet if knowledge can be no substitute for faith in this life, in the end it is superior because even mysteries, which are not properly objects of knowledge in this life, are ultimately knowable *secundum rationem*, not *contra rationem*. Lastly, in the area of epistemology Hugh seems to have made no significant contributions.[5]

At the apex of Hugh's thought is mystical activity, by which through the supernatural influence of grace over our sin-weakened faculties we can gradually ascend to the contemplation of God in Himself. Thus mysticism crowns the ascent of knowledge in this existence as the beatific vision of God crowns it in heaven; whereas philosophical and theological knowledge is knowledge *about* God, mystical activity entails the direct and loving knowledge *of* God. Yet this activity is not the same as the Beatific Vision to be had in heaven, despite its supremacy in this life among the kinds of knowledge, for in the mystical experience the soul here and now is incapable of comprehending the fulness of God's presence.

His major works are the *Didascalion*,[6] an encyclopedia of profane and sacred knowledge designed as an introduction to philosophical study, and

---

[4] See Copleston, *History of Philosophy* II, 176-177.

[5] E. Gilson, *History of Christian Philosophy*, 171 and 634, where he cites and approves the conclusions of J. Kleinz, *The Theory of Knowledge of Hugh of Saint Victor* (Washington, 1944) 50-55, and 61, concerning Hugh's treatment of the problem of abstraction.

[6] *Publications of the Modern Language Association* 67 (April 1953) 240, notes a translation of the *Didascalion* to be in progress by Jerome Taylor as a dissertation at the University of Chicago.

the *De sacramentis Christianae fidei*,[7] a prelude to the *Summas* of the
following centuries. In *Didascalion* Hugh devotes three books to the
liberal arts and three to religious questions. He states three conditions
for the acquisition of knowledge: natural talent (*natura*), study (*lectio*
and *meditatio*) and zeal (*disciplina*) and he makes four divisions of
profane knowledge: *theoretica* (theology, mathematics, and physics)
which seeks to discover truth, *practica* (ethics, economics, and politics)
which considers moral problems, mechanics, including such disparate
topics as weaving and medicine, and logic. This last includes grammar
and discourse, which subdivides into demonstration, rhetoric, and dialec-
tics.[8] The seven liberal arts within the framework of the *trivium* and
*quadrivium* form an inseparable unity and they must all be mastered before one can truly philosophize. In *De sacramentis* Hugh views the whole
universe in the light of the sacraments of the Church and sees the world
as pregnant with divine significance. The central moments of the univer-
sal history of the world are the creation and the Incarnation, and the
sacramental system is the central light which makes possible an interpre-
tation of the world along specifically Christian lines, in accordance with
the Augustinian doctrine that the world reveals God in varying degrees
of fulness.[9] For Hugh and the Victorine school in general the whole system of creation leads up to man, and then from man and in man to
Christ, at once the human and divine representative of our unseen Father
in heaven. The heart of religion and of life is to see everything in Christ
and to see Him *clarificatum*, in perfect clarity. Hugh maintained it is
possible to perceive God as revealed in the created order and to receive
thereby the divine grace which such perception brings. In preparation
for this great privilege all the pious practices of religion are to be utilized,
for they make possible this perception and reception of the Deity.
Strengthened and purified by the sacramental resources of the Church
the soul may then contemplate its God. This contemplation is the end and
goal of all human endeavor. for God's wisdom as revealed in creation is
the *janua et via* to the knowledge of His invisible nature, and it is through
contemplation of the visible, regarded as the manifestations of God, that
we take our first steps towards knowing Him in the fulness of His Being
through direct adoration. But we may even do more than know Him, for
through the sacraments we can receive Him as He is.

## II. THE MYSTIC

Mysticism (from the root *my*, which means to shut up or close) in

---

[8] For various topics treated in *Didascalion* see E. Gilson, *History of Christian Philosophy*, 634, n. 121.
[9] This analysis of *De sacramentis* derives from W. Pittenger, "The Incarnational
Philosophy of Hugh of St. Victor," *Theology* 31 (1935) 274-278.
[7] Roy J. Deferrari, *On the Sacraments of the Christian Faith* (Cambridge, Mass.,
1951), is an English translation of this work.

[5]

general signifies a tendency to seek a union with God in an intimate and hidden way. Understood in this sense mysticism is closely connected to religion, for when religion flourishes it also does, and when religious fervor fails so also does mystical practice.[10] Consequently there is no cause for wonder that the twelfth century, an age of ardent faith, saw the practice and development of all forms of mysticism. There were the practical, the autobiographical, and the speculative mystics, these last being especially devoted to developing theory by the method of introspection. They described the states which bring about in varying degree direct communion between the soul and God, and some even sought to explain the world of reality in terms of such a union. Gilson recognizes two groups of theologians in this century who initiated and conducted the movement of theological speculation on love: the Cistercian school founded by St. Bernard and William of St. Thierry and the Victorine school, established by Hugh and continued by successors such as Richard.[11] Inherent in both of these schools are a number of principles which guided their speculation. First, the communion with God is the result of love and requires contemplation which will reveal his majesty and greatness. This activity is fulfilled in the joyous and peaceful possession of God. Secondly, this communion is based on a direct and immediate intuition and not on ordinary or analogical knowledge. Lastly, this union of God and the soul is the culminating point of all psychic activity.[12]

Among the sources of the mystical schools of the twelfth century might be named the *Confessions* of St. Augustine, the works of Clement of Alexandria and Pseudo-Dionysius, the *De institutione coenobiorum* of Cassian, and the *De vita contemplativa* attributed to Prosper of Aquitaine. But whatever sources may have influenced him, Hugh's particular contribution was to develop a speculative mysticism based on a solid respect for learning and aimed at a codification, as it were, of the laws governing the soul's journey to God. His approach should be especially attractive to those moderns who are inclined to think of mysticism as escapism at worst and a kind of monomania at best. His balanced judgment maintained that on the one hand ignorance was weakness and hatred of learning a sign of depravity, but on the other that the objects of our search for knowledge should be truth and goodness, and ultimately God and our salvation. His reasoned combination of philosophy, dialectical theology, and mysticism is a rarity in any age.

Scholars have distinguished two kinds of speculative mysticism, ac-

---

[10] See M. DeWulf, *History of Mediaeval Philosophy* I (London, 1926) 209.

[11] E. Gilson, *History of Christian Philosophy*, 164-171.

[12] DeWulf, *History of Mediaeval Philosophy* I, 210; for some specific differences in the mystical way, see the analysis of Gilson, *History of Christian Philosophy*, 164-171, pertaining to St. Bernard, William of St. Thierry, Isaac of Stella, Alcher of Clairvaux, and Hugh and Richard of St. Victor.

cording to the nature of the union between the soul and God. Pluralistic or individualistic mysticism maintains that in this most intimate activity the knowing and loving soul remains distinct from its God, whereas monistic or pantheistic mysticism holds that in some way or other the soul at this time is identified with the Divine Being. A further extension of these categories are the terms natural and supernatural mysticism as applied respectively to the above classes. Those who maintain a substantial distinction exists in this union also deny that the soul of itself and without the free gift of grace can attain to God in a sufficiently intimate and direct manner. On the contrary, this gift of grace is unnecessary for those who identify the soul and God in this union. For them this activity is the highest manifestation of psychic life in this natural existence. Rousselot in his study of the problem of mystical love analyzed the nature rather than the mode of it.[13] He distinguishes between what he calls the physical or natural conception and the ecstatic conception. The former sees the essence of love in the disposition of every created being to seek its own good; in loving God man does not cease to love himself, for God is our greatest good and final end. This is the approach of Hugh in the *De Sacramentis* (2, 13-14; PL 176, 528-550, esp. 531-534). The ecstatic conception holds that the lover comes forth from himself, as it were, to be absorbed utterly in the Beloved. It is a view which is found to some extent in Richard of St. Victor, Hugh's most famous successor at the abbey, in the Cistercians, the followers of Abelard, and even in Hugh and St. Bernard. Vernet points out that the terms used for these distinctions are not very apt and that these two concepts interpenetrate in a way which makes hard and fast divisions difficult. Some light is cast on the problem if it be noted that the first deals with the metaphysical aspect, the second with the psychological aspect of love. The *De arrha animae* is most interesting in this regard because it begins with the acceptance of the physical conception on a purely natural level, then as the Soul is informed this is extended to the divine, and finally near the end of the work the burning devotion of Man and his Soul, the interlocutors, shades into the ecstatic conception.

Hugh can be called a mystic in a number of senses. If by this term is meant the inclination to believe that the love of the good and purity of soul prepare for the pursuit of knowledge, Hugh is a mystic, for he affirms the necessity of moral integrity for one who would philosophize profitably. (*Didascalion* 1, 2-3; 3, 13-20; PL 176, 742-743; 773-778). Again, if mysticism consists in the habit of prayer, of reflection and mortification, and in the superiority attributed to works of love over specu-

---

[13] P. Rousselot, "Pour l'histoire du problème de l'amour au moyen âge," *Beiträge zur Geschichte der Philosophie des Mittelalters* VI, 6 (Münster i. W. 1908); see the short analysis in F. Vernet, *Medieval Spirituality* (London, 1930) 177-178.

lative knowledge in the quest for perfection, the ascetical works of Hugh prove him a mystic (e.g., *De institutione novitiorum, PL* 176, 925-952). But properly speaking, the use of the word *mystic* in each of these cases is invalid, for the doctrine of the importance of the purification of the soul to acquire truth is of a philosophical order, and the science of Christian perfection pertains to ascetical theology. Mystical theology is another matter.[14]

Mystical activity can bring it about that God will enter into the existence of a soul in an extraordinary manner, and by the influence of exceptional grace raise it to a knowledge and love far above the ordinary. In this condition is to be found the fulness of mysticism. Hugh is a mystical theologian because, not content to examine the method of ordinary perfection, he describes the mystical ascent. In this regard, perhaps no better work of his than the present one could be selected to illustrate this particular relationship between the soul and God. For Hugh there are five degrees on the road to perfection: learning, reflection, prayer, action, and contemplation. Of the last named there are two kinds, acquired or active, and passive or infused, but these specific terms are not employed by him. The former might be called meditation, the latter contemplation proper. Active contemplation considers all creation as its object and it results in awe and wonderment. In passive contemplation on the other hand the soul observes its Creator in a most intimate manner and in union with God it is in some way transformed by the flame of the divine love. It is enveloped by divinity and in possession of truth and perfect charity it takes its rest in a supreme calm, seeking nothing beyond its proper good.

In explaining his views concerning the nature of this contemplation of the Creator, Hugh maintains that prior to the orginal sin Adam possessed a threefold faculty for knowledge. (*De sacramentis* 1, 10, 2; *PL* 176, 329). These were the eye of the body, by which he saw the physical universe; the eye of reason, by which his soul gained knowledge of self; and the eye of contemplation, by which the soul viewed God and things divine. By original sin the last of these faculties was lost, the eye of reason was badly weakened, and only the physical power of sight was left intact. As a result, man could continue to view the physical universe as before, but his own soul was now only dimly recognizable and the sight of God had utterly vanished. Hence faith becomes an absolute necessity for man if he is to believe in what is no longer visible. The nature and extent of man's perception of God before the fall is set forth in *De sacramentis* (1, 6, 14; *PL* 176, 271). Man then knew his Creator not by any external means but by an inner perception; not by faith but

---

[14] See Vernet, *Dictionnaire*, 263-266, for the above and much of what follows.

rather by contemplating God as known and present. This knowledge was greater and more certain than that which now comes from faith, yet less than that which will result when the Beatific Vision is beheld. It is this intuition which the soul can regain with extraordinary grace by means of the eye of contemplation. How is this perception to be distinguished from the Beatific Vision? All that can be said is that it is neither a clouded and transient *visio Dei per essentiam* nor is it a perception of God by means of phantasms, inferences, or other discursive means.

Contemplation therefore terminates in love. In a passage on the homilies in *Ecclesiastes* (*In Ecclesiasten homiliae* XIX, 1; *PL* 175, 117-118) Hugh says that after continual contemplation of the truth, the human heart as if wholly inflamed enters into the very center of supreme truth and there rests at peace, apart from all disturbance and confusion. For him the *Canticle of Canticles* is *the* book of contemplation: in *Proverbs* Solomon began with reflection, in *Ecclesiastes* he arose to the first step of contemplation, *i.e.*, acquired, and in the *Canticle of Canticles* he reached the second and final step, *i.e.*, infused knowledge of his God. Hugh's classic statement on the superiority of love is worth noticing at this point, for love is the motivating force of the mystical ascent and in a more perfect mode it also becomes the result of the ascent. He says that love surpasses knowledge and is greater than understanding, for we love more than we understand and love draws near and enters where knowledge remains outside. (*Expositio in Hierarchiam Coelestem S. Dionysii Areopagitae* 6; *PL* 175, 1038). Thomas Gallus, Tauler, Ruysbroeck, John of Schoohoven, Rudolph of Biberach, Gerson, and Vincent of Aggsbach were to reiterate this view and Richard of St. Victor, William of St. Thierry, and St. Bonaventure expressed it in similar terms.[15]

The mysticism of Hugh is not pantheistic, ontologistic, idealistic in the neo-Platonic sense, nor quietistic. It is not the first since it does not identify the soul and God, nor is it the second for Hugh teaches that we do not naturally see God, but that by an extraordinary favor there sometimes occurs a certain perception of Him which is distinct from the Beatific Vision. Thirdly, it is not neo-Platonic pantheism, although Hugh certainly was influenced by the Pseudo-Areopagite and by St. Augustine. He wrote a commentary on the *Celestial Hierarchy* of the former and from the latter he took his theory of knowledge, according to which God plays in our knowledge the role which Aristotelians attribute to the agent intellect. Whatever the intrinsic value of the Augustinian theory, it is a view of natural, not mystical knowledge, and if the commentary on the *Celestial Hierarchy* reflects neo-Platonic conceptions, it is nevertheless orthodox in the view of some scholars.[16] Lastly, the mysticism of Hugh

---

[15] Vernet, *Medieval Spirituality*, 159.
[16] Vernet, *Dictionnaire*, 265, for all of the above analysis.

is not quietism, for it does not make of mystical contemplation a perpetual act or state, but rather a necessarily transitory condition. It also requires the practice of the virtues and a regard for works which quietists consider unworthy of the soul which has reached this high state. In sum, his mysticism depends on no extraordinary experiences or sudden revelations from on high. By the use of allegory and similar techniques of extension and persuasion he guides the soul in a rational manner to effective contemplation and so by means of God's grace to a direct experience of his Creator in that peace and joy which surpasses understanding.

### III. The Mystical Works

Hugh has not left in the fields of ascetical and mystical theology a work of the scope of *De sacramentis*.[17] He wrote two works for religious on the principles of asceticism, *De institutione novitiorum* (*PL* 176, 925-952) and *Expositio in regulam B. Augustini* (*PL* 176, 881-924). The former is more concerned with manners than with virtue and the latter discusses the rule of St. Augustine adopted by the canons of St. Victor. In the exegetical work *In Solomonis Ecclesiasten homiliae XIX* (*PL* 175, 113-256) he begins with a description of the process of contemplation. *De arca Noe morali* (*PL* 176, 617-680), *De arca Noe mystica* (*PL* 176, 681-704), and *De vanitate mundi* (*PL* 176, 704-740) form a trilogy of a sort, wherein we first see man fallen away from the contemplation of God. The cause for this is love of the world and the remedy is love of God. To achieve this end it is necessary for man to detach himself from the affairs of this transient existence and seek God by means of the ark of salvation. This idea embraces the Church, the gift of grace, and man's own determination. He must use this ark to return to God by means of contemplation and good deeds. In the mystical ascent meditation plays an important role and Hugh has accordingly devoted the little work *De meditando* (*PL* 176, 993-998) to this topic. He also treats of the subject in the *Didascalion* (*PL* 176, 772; 835); in this passage there is the noteworthy view that from the knowledge of visible things we ascend to that of our Creator, then from the knowledge of God we return to that of our own soul, of other men, and of the lower creatures. Next to meditation is prayer, occasioned by the misery of man and the mercy of our Redeemer, a subject treated in *De modo orandi* (*PL* 176, 977). *De laude charitatis* (*PL* 176, 969-976) is a panegyric on charity and the brief work *De amore sponsi ad sponsam* (*PL* 176, 987-994) repeats some of the ideas treated at greater length in the *Soliloquium*. *De contemplatione*, not included in the *Patrologia Latina*, considers the degrees and modes of contemplation; Haureau thought it a genuine work of Hugh, but Vernet expresses hesi-

---

[17] Vernet, *Dictionnaire*, 287-289, for a more complete treatment of what follows here.

tation to accept it as such.[18] Lastly, Hugh's *chef-d'oeuvre* in the field of mystical theology is the *Soliloquium de arrha animae*, truly a little gem both in content and in style. (*PL* 176, 951-970).

## IV. THE SOLILOQUY ON THE EARNEST MONEY OF THE SOUL

Since this work is actually a dialogue between a man and his soul, the title at first sight seems to be rather odd. However, in the Middle Ages the terms *dialogue* and *soliloquy* were in certain cases synonymous in literature; the latter could be used to describe a dialogue between a man and his soul or a man and God. The word *arrha* originally signified what we call a down payment, but in Middle Latin it came to designate those gifts which are given at the time of betrothal. Critical opinion of the style and treatment of the *Soliloquy* has been almost wholly favorable.[19] Stylistically the work might truly be called an *aureus libellus*, just as the *Dialogus de oratoribus* of Tacitus was so named in antiquity. The popularity of the work is testified to by the many French versions of it that were circulated in the following centuries. There were others in Flemish, Catalan, and German.

The purpose of the work is to direct the soul toward a true love of self, an attitude which is identical with a love of God. This is in accordance with the Augustinian formula that God loves him who truly loves himself. The dramatic development of the discourse is clear and simple. To persuade the soul that true self-esteem is ultimately better for it than all the ephemeral objects to which it is presently attracted, the writer shows that the soul itself is far more worthy of love. He does this by demonstrating that the soul is the object of divine love and that in fact God has already presented the pledge of His love. In the order of creation this promise is to be seen in the subordination of all creatures and things to the service of man; in the order of redemption, in the calling of the Christian to spiritual perfection. The nature of true self-esteem therefore consists in seeking for the Supreme Good, a task which can only be achieved through self-examination and contemplation. Further, the passage from sensible objects to self-knowledge to the first glimpse of that Good can only be made by the way of grace and spiritual exercises. To realize all this and then to undertake the task of preparation constitutes the acceptance by the soul of the pledge of Divine Love. This willing response to the advances of the invisible Lover is a token that some day this love will be consummated in heaven, even if it is now only

---

[18] Vernet, *Dictionnaire*, 288.
[19] M. Ledrus, "Hugues de St.-Victor: Le gage des divines fiançailles (*De arrha animae*) traduite et annoté," *Museum Lessianum: Section ascetique et mystique*, No. 12 (Louvain 1923), 9-56, gives a complete treatment of the work in all its aspects and relates it to the whole of Hugh's thought; see K. Müller, "Zur Mystik Hugos von St. Viktor," *Zeitschrift für Kirchengeschichte* 45 (1926) 175-189, for a shorter examination.

dimly perceived and intermittently enjoyed.[20] To paraphrase Hugh's own words: *Sponsus erit Deus, sponsa erit anima.*

The exposition is in accord with scholastic principles. First the natural love of God is awakened in the soul and repentance follows by means of grace. The reception of the sacraments and spiritual exercises then make possible the rise of the soul toward perfection in order to prepare for the mystical union. This description of the mystical ascent is not predicated upon an eternal relationship of the soul to divinity, as in neo-Platonism, but rather upon the means of grace within the Church, and so upon the historical mission of Christ himself. Essentially the *Soliloquy* is a meditation upon the divine benevolence. The greatest requital the soul can offer to this is the sincere desire and effort to become worthy of the possession of its Lover.

In conclusion, a few words about the literary devices used in the work. The very nature of the experience which the mystic attempts to describe makes it advisable for him to use figures which will concretize and vivify his ideas. To this end Hugh uses personification, historical analogy, allegory, tropology, and simile. Perhaps the most striking figure to modern tastes is the passage wherein the soul is warned of insincerity by the description of the harlot. The thorough diagnosis of her degradation is clinical in its approach. The symbolic method is to be seen in the title itself and in the pervasive theme that all creation serves as the pledge-money of the Divine Suitor's love for the soul. Lastly, the intensity and climactic character of the language of love in the concluding paragraphs subtly conveys the notion of the feeling which the soul now bears for its Lover. This idea is realistically sustained at the very end by the final note of calm and satisfaction.

---

[20] Ledrus, "Hugues . . .," pp. 22-23.

# Hugh of St. Victor
## Soliloquy on the Earnest Money of the Soul

### PROLOGUE

To our beloved Brother G and to the other servants of Christ at Hamersleben, greetings. Hugh, servant of your holiness, such as he is, desires you to walk together in peace and come to the same repose. I am submitting to your kindness a soliloquy on love, entitled *On the Earnest Money of the Soul*, that you may learn where you should seek true love and how you ought to arouse in your hearts a desire for heavenly joys by zeal in spiritual meditations. And so, dearest Brother, I ask that with all the others you accept this work as a souvenir of its author. In sending it especially to you I do not intend thereby to exclude the others, nor in offering it to the entire community would I have you think it less your gift. I do not intend here to attract your attention with the pretense of a learned work; rather I write because I cannot conceal my devotion to you. Give greetings to Brothers B and A and all the others whose names, although I am unable to mention them here singly, I greatly desire to see written in the Book of Life. Farewell.

### SOLILOQUY

Man:[1]   In secret I shall speak to my soul and in friendly conversation I shall obtain what I desire to know. No other person will be admitted, but by ourselves we shall converse in complete candor. In that way I shall not fear to ask of hidden matters nor will my soul be ashamed to respond with the truth.

Tell me, my soul, what is it that you love above all things? I know that love is your very life and that without love you cannot exist. But I wish that without any timidity you would reveal to me what among all things you have chosen as the object of your affection. In order that you may more clearly understand, I shall explain what it is I ask you. Look at the universe and all the things which it contains. There you will find many beautiful and alluring forms which attract human desires and which, according to the variety of delight to be had by their users, inflame men's appetites to enjoy them. Gold has its splendor, stones theirs; the human form its beauty, tapestries and purple vestments their color. The number of such things is infinite; so why catalogue them for you?

---

[1] The critical edition of the text by M. K. Müller (Bonn, 1913), that in *PL*, and the edition of Rouen (1648) leave undetermined the identity of the person (*Homo*) who converses with his soul. The *editio princeps* and the MS. of Schöntal show *Hugo* in place of *Homo*, and the scholars Haureau and Ledrus prefer this usage.

Indeed you also are acquainted with all these things; you have seen almost each one individually, and very many have you experienced. Many you recall already having seen, and many you still see, and in these you could experience and confirm what I say. Show me then, I beseech you, which of all these you have made the single object which alone you would wish to embrace and could enjoy forever; for I am certain you are taken with some one of these things you see, or if you have already put all of these aside, you have some other which you love more than all these.[2]

*His Soul:* As I am unable to love what I have never seen, so to the present time I have been unable to love any of all those things which are visible, nor have I yet found among all these things that which ought to be loved above all else. Indeed I have learned by many trials that a love of this world is ephemeral and deceptive, an affection which I must always abandon when what I have chosen passes away, or change when something more pleasing surpasses it. And so thus far I vacillate among my desires while I am able neither to exist without love nor to find a true devotion.

*Man:* I am happy that at least you are not fixed in a love of temporal things, but I grieve that you do not yet rest in a love of eternal goods. You would be very unhappy if in exile you made your home, but now, since you do wander abroad, there is need to recall you to the true way. You would surely make your home in exile if in this transitory existence you determined to take an everlasting love. Indeed, you are now wandering in exile because, while you are attracted by a desire for temporal goods you cannot find a love of those things which are eternal.[3] But an important beginning for salvation is in your power, for you have learned

[2] On the subject of meditation, which occupies the greatest part of the soliloquy, see *De meditando, PL* 176, 993. It consists in "assiduous reflection, applied to a consideration of the manner, cause, and meaning of each thing." The *De arrha* gives us three kinds of meditation: that of creatures inspired by positive knowledge, that of Holy Scripture, and lastly that of conduct.

[3] The mutability of the conditions of our earthly existence has vividly stirred the spirit of this man so familiar with the serenity of the intellectual life. It seems to him that this situation is characteristic of the fallen state of man. "Since man has allowed his concupiscence to turn himself toward the multiple and the transitory, he has lost his stability; he loves many things and his heart is divided among them. He gives himself to the pursuit of transient goods and he is always changing his desires. He is another Cain, 'a wanderer and a fugitive upon the earth.' In his wanderings he seeks here, now there, for consolation; a fugitive, he seeks to avoid affliction. He is always on the move, but as this continues he grows weak. He sits down then or he remains standing in order not to grow faint. Nevertheless, if he continues in this manner he grows weak, too. We grow weak from hunger and then we eat in order not to perish; yet if we eat unceasingly we shall perish. What we seek for our happiness is turned to our sorrow; thus every change of man is a fault, not an improvement; we grow weak because we are always going from this to that, and we never stop in order not to grow weak." *De sacramentis,* 1, 9, 3; *PL* 176, 320-321 A; *cf. De vanitate mundi,* 2; *PL,* 176, 711.

[14]

to change your love to the better object. Hence you will be able to be separated from all love of finite things if a greater beauty be shown you which you would more gladly embrace.

*His Soul:*   How is it possible to reveal what cannot be seen? Furthermore, how is it possible to love the invisible? Surely if in temporal and visible matters there is to be found no true and abiding affection, and if the invisible cannot be loved, an unending misery pursues an immortal being when a lasting love cannot be discovered. No one indeed can be happy without love, for in this alone is it agreed that unhappiness consists: not to esteem what one is. Who would call that man happy or even human who forgetful of mankind and spurning the comforts of society loves himself alone with a certain solitary and miserable delight? Therefore it is necessary that you either approve the love of what is visible, or if you eliminate this that you reveal something else which can be loved more profitably and agreeably.

*Man:*   If you therefore believe that the temporal and the visible ought to be loved because you see therein a certain beauty natural to them, why do you not esteem yourself instead, you who in your comeliness surpass the grace and beauty of all visible things? If you could but see yourself, if you could observe your own countenance, you would surely know what great reproof you deserved in thinking some physical object external to yourself worthy of your love.

*His Soul:*   The eye sees all, but it does not see itself; by this light whereby we discern all other things we do not see our own visage, in which the light has been placed. By other means do men perceive their faces, and they learn of the aspect of the countenance more often by words than by sight, unless you bring forth a certain mirror of another kind, by which I can know and love the sight of my heart. For would not everyone rightly call that man foolish who for the purpose of nourishing his love should continually consider his own likeness in a mirror? Therefore, since I cannot consider my own face and the quality of my countenance, I very easily extend my affection to external things which seem to be admirable, especially since love never permits itself to be solitary. For it somehow ceases to exist if it does not pour forth the ardor of its affection upon a companion of equal station.

*Man:*   He is not alone who is in the company of God, nor is the vigor of love extinguished if its appetite is restrained from the vile and the base. That man does a very great injury to himself who admits to the company of his love what is either dishonorable or unworthy. First, therefore, there is need for each man to consider himself, and when he has come to recognize his own dignity, he should not become attached to things inferior to himself lest he injure his own love. For things which in

[15]

themselves are beautiful lose their worth when compared to more graceful objects. And just as it is unfit to join the deformed to the beautiful, so it is utterly unbecoming to join to the most seemly that which has no fairness unless it be of an imaginary or inferior order. Do not desire a love that is solitary or degraded, my Soul. You seek one that will be yours alone; search also for one that is especially worthy.

You know that love is a fire and that fire seeks its touchwood in order to burn. But beware lest you cast on it what results more in a smoke or a stench. This is the force of love, that it is necessary for you to be such as the one you cherish. Somehow by the association of love you are transformed to the likeness of the very one to whom you are joined by affection. Consider, my Soul, your own charm and you will then perceive what sort of beauty you ought to desire. Your countenance is not hidden from you and your eye sees nothing well if it does not discern itself. For since it is obviously suited for contemplating itself, no foreign likeness nor empty shadow of the truth can deceive it. If by chance that internal vision of yours has grown dull through negligence and you cannot observe yourself as is fitting and advantageous, why do you not then depend on another's judgment concerning what you ought to think about yourself![4]

You have a betrothed but you do not know it. He is the most comely of all, but you have not seen his face. He, however, does see you, for if he did not, he would not love you. As yet he has not wished to present himself to you, but he has sent his gifts and given the pledge money, the bond of his love and the sign of his fervor. If you could recognize him and see his face, you would no longer be in doubt about your own fairness; you would know indeed that one so beautiful, handsome, dignified, and extraordinary as he would not have been captivated by you unless a singular comeliness in you, admirable beyond that of others, had attracted him.[5] What therefore will you do? Now you are unable to see him because he is absent. And so do you neither fear nor blush to do him injury, since you scorn his wholly devoted love and prostitute yourself shamefully and immodestly to some harmful pleasure? Do not so conduct yourself!

[4] Hugh considers knowledge of self as an object of faith for the Christian who is not yet freed from his desires (Ostler, *Die Psychologie*, 137). Before attaining to the wisdom which permits him to contemplate his intellectual nature, man ought to recognize and admit the evidence immediately before him. This attitude of faith is analogous to that which results in the contemplation of God.

[5] "Marriage, instituted before the original sin, is the symbol of the spiritual relation which exists between God and the soul, as a result of love, . . . and between Christ and the Church, as a result of the Incarnation. In every way the bridegroom is superior; his love is given through benevolence to one less than he; the bride is in every way inferior and cannot suffice of herself. For this reason her love is turned of necessity toward one above her." *De sacramentis*, 1, 8, 13; *PL* 176, 314-315.

If up to now you have been unable to know what manner of person he is who holds you dear, consider at least the pledge money which he has given. Perhaps by his very gift you will be able to perceive with what affection you ought to love him and with what zeal and diligence you ought to preserve yourself unsullied for him. His pledge-gift is superb, a worthy present, for it did not become his greatness that he give small things nor his wisdom that he give great gifts for small. Great, therefore, is that which he has given to you, but greater yet is that which he loves in you. Great, therefore, is his gift. What has your betrothed given you, my Soul? Perhaps you are expectant but unaware of what I shall say. You consider those from whom you have received anything of value and you do not find that you possess or have received anything like this about which you might now boast. And so I shall tell you so that you may know what your betrothed has given you.

Look at the universe and consider whether there is anything in it which does not serve you. All nature directs its course to the end that it may serve your desires, be subject to your use, and unceasingly meet both your pleasures and your needs. This the heavens, earth, seas and all things in them never fail to supply. To this the turn of the seasons, with their annual renewals and revived offspring, gives an unending sustenance, renewing the old, re-establishing the fallen, and restoring the worn. Now who do you think established this? Who directs all nature that with one accord it should be at your service? You accept the benefit but you do not know your benefactor. The gift is plain to see, but the giver is hidden. And yet reason itself does not allow you to have any doubt that all this is not your due and that it is a gift from someone. Therefore, whoever that one is, he has given you very much in granting you all these blessings.

Greatly must he be loved who can bestow so much, and the fact that he desired to give so generously proves his own great love. By his gift he is revealed as one who loves and is worthy of being loved greatly. Not to respond to such a lover is wicked and perverse as not to gladly desire such a lover is foolish. Look, therefore, rash and imprudent Soul, look at what you are doing, since in this world you desire to love and be loved. All the universe is subject to you and there is hardly anything in it which excels in beauty, usefulness, size, or quality that you do not gladly accept. If you truly love these things, love them as being subject to you, love them as objects at your service, as the earnest money of your betrothed, as the offerings of a true friend, as the benefactions of a master. In order that you may always remember what you owe to him, do not prefer these gifts to the giver, but hold them dear because of him and through and above them love him. My Soul, take care lest, heaven forbid, you be called harlot rather than beloved, should you prefer the gifts of the giver more than the affection of the lover. You do a greater injury to his devotion if you also accept his gifts but do not requite his love. Spurn his gifts if you are able, or if you cannot, return your love for his. Love him, respect yourself, and honor his gifts for his sake. Love him that you may take your joy in him; esteem yourself because you are loved by him; delight in his gifts because they have been given by him. Love him for your own and keep yourself for him; rejoice in his gifts because they have been given you by him for your own sake. This is truly a pure and chaste affection, having nothing that is sordid, bitter, or ephemeral, and being comely in its purity, pleasing in its sweetness, and lasting in its duration.

*His Soul:* Your words have inflamed me; I am now ardent and deeply stirred within. Although I have not seen him who you say is so lovable, still I confess that by the very sweetness of your description and the gentleness of your persuasion you are kindling in me a love of him. Indeed, I am forced by your arguments to cherish him above all, from whom I now see I have received everything as a pledge of his devotion. Yet there remains one thing which could greatly lessen the joy of this love, unless the hand of your consolation removes this hindrance as it has all else.

*Man:* I truly promise you there is in this love nothing which can rightly cause you sadness. And yet, lest I seem more to deceive your trust than give witness to the truth, I wish you would tell me what disturbs you, so that again strengthened by my words you may grow even stronger in your desire for him.

*His Soul:* I wish you would recall (and I believe you have not forgotten) that a little while ago when you were commending a true and honorable love, you said that it ought to be unique not only in its devotion but also in its choice, that is, dedicated to the beloved only and only to one who ought to be loved. For a love is not perfectly praiseworthy if another one with the beloved is desired or if one is cherished who is not supremely worthy. You see, therefore, that I love one who is especially chosen and loved alone. But my devotion suffers this wrong, for though I love him only I am not his only delight. You yourself recognize the numbers and the types there are with whom I share this pledge of his devotion. How then shall I be able to glory in this privilege, so great a gift as you say, if it is possessed in common not only with the brutes but with all living things? What greater boon does the light of the sun confer on me than on the reptiles and the worms of the earth? All creatures live alike and breathe alike; there is the same nourishment, the same drink for all. What is so great or singular in this? Surely you see what sort of problem this is. Therefore, you do not prove with sufficient point your contention that he alone is to be loved if you do not also show him

[18]

at least in some manner singularly devoted. Yet I admit these gifts are great and they would be worthy of complete requital if they had been given only to one.

*Man:* Your earnestness is not displeasing since it is evident that in seeking so eagerly the cause of perfect love you also desire to give your love with complete devotion. So I am glad to undertake this discussion with you in order to defend the devotion of this best of lovers from that charge of which you speak and also set you aright lest by some suspicion you waver in your choice of him. To begin, there are three matters which cause you concern. Consider the gifts which you have received from your betrothed: some have been given to you in common with others, some to you as one of a special group, and some to you as yours alone. The first class serves all creatures both for your sake and in common with you; the second serves many though not all, also for your sake and in common with you; and the third has been granted to you alone. Does your lover then honor you the less because he has bestowed certain of his gifts on everyone as well as you? Would he have made you happy if he had given the world to you alone? Suppose there were no men or beasts upon the earth and that you possessed its riches in solitude! Where then would be the pleasing and needful fellowship of human intercourse? Where the delights and comforts you now enjoy? Consider then that in this also he did much for you because he created these things for your comfort. If this world and all things in it do you service, in what way have they not all been created for your use? Does the head of a family alone eat his bread or take his drink? Is he alone clothed in his garments and warmed at his hearth? Does he alone dwell in his house? Yet not without reason is he said to possess everything that is used by those who reside with him, either under the law of love or of subjection. And so, whether something serves you directly or is necessary for those under you, everything has been given to you and awaits your disposal.

*His Soul:* You have reduced rather than removed what was troubling me. For I was complaining of this, that though loving truly I was not loved alike in return, for I have seen the pledge of this love equally granted to others. Yet your arguments have convinced me that those gifts have been personally granted to me which I see given in common with those at my service. I concede that you have spoken sufficiently on this point, but I do not do so concerning the matter which was disturbing me. I have learned that everything by which lower life is sustained is to be assigned to my custody, because those things which in turn are nourished by it have been disposed for my use. Yet the privilege of a singular love is not demonstrated thereby, because these things have not been granted to me alone but to all men alike and to many quite amply. Therefore, in regard to all these gifts which have been granted for the use of men in common, even though certain ones may unjustly claim something more for themselves, those are in error who consider anything to be given solely to their custody. Thus there is a certain special love of the Creator toward men in which they can glory more fully than other creatures. Yet no man is better than any other in this. In your assertion about a singular love, that among other things the society of men has been granted to me, I can find nothing distinctive since all share mutually in this benefit. In this society not only the lost glory of distinction but also the commonness of participation causes me sorrow. How many are the unbelievers, the criminals, and the lechers in this society who can also boast of this?

*Man:* It ought not to disturb you that in the use of temporal goods there is the same participation both for the good and the wicked, nor on that account should you think the latter are similarly loved by God since you see them share these blessings with you. For just as the beasts have been created not for their own sake but for man's, so also do evil men live for the sake of the good and not for their own. And as their lives serve by example for the welfare of the good, there can be no doubt that everything which nourishes their existence is also to be considered as under the dominion of the just. The wicked are permitted to live among the good in order that their association may stimulate the lives of the virtuous. In their good fortune they are a warning to seek goods which are lasting and cannot be known by evil men, and in their iniquity they cause the good to seek virtue more resolutely. Lastly, when the good see these wretches, bereft of divine grace, plunging into every depth of vice, they may learn what great thanks they owe to their Creator for their own salvation. Indeed, the plan of divine providence requires these means to guard our salvation and to reveal to us our future glory. Just as from the life of the brutes we see that supreme happiness is not to be had in using the goods of this world, so also from the lives of wicked men we can perceive that it cannot be had in giving ourselves up to these things. And so these gifts must be granted to good and wicked alike since otherwise the good would not believe that better things were in store for them, unless they saw these present advantages to be common to good and bad alike. Therefore, complain no more about this forced companionship and the good fortune of the wicked nor consider them joined with you in the privilege of this unique love, for they are your fellows in the use and possession of merely transient things. They also are of assistance to your salvation, as we have said, because they not only use these gifts of creation but they are dominated by them.

But what shall I say of the companionship of good men? This one point now remains to be considered, whether on this account you cannot boast of the complete devotion of your lover since you are not loved by him apart from the company of all just men. Because of this I wish you would recall that opinion which I mentioned above and which you believed not very suitable for proving the point in discussion. Hence I repeat it here in order more earnestly to discuss with you whether in any way the truth of the matter can be stated for confirming what we seek to show. I said that the company of good men was a gift of the Creator to you so that you might take comfort from it and not be wearied by a solitary and miserable existence. And so as the lives of the wicked are a constant warning to you, the lives of the virtuous are your consolation. They are surely so helpful that you should not spurn them as participants in your blessings or as equals in this love. For if you truly love the virtuous, whatever blessing comes to them makes the charity which is in you rejoice as though the benefit were yours and not another's. Indeed it would be blessed to enjoy this love alone, but it is much more blessed to delight in it in the company of the many good men in this life. In sharing this affection with them the joys of your charity and magnanimity are redoubled.

The love of the spirit, in effect, is more perfectly known to each man when it is shared by all. It is not lessened by this participation of many, for its delights are realized completely and uniquely by each of them. And so in no way does the companionship of the good infringe upon the privilege of your singular love, for your espoused loves you in all others who are cherished for your sake. By this means he shows his devotion in a special manner because he loves nothing apart from you. Do not fear then that his love will be divided by his affection for the many and so will be less ardent toward individuals because it seems somehow to be apportioned and divided among the many. He is present to each one as he is to all, for he would give neither a special nor a greater affection to individuals if he should love them apart from others. Therefore, let everyone love him with all their hearts that they may so be cherished by him. For no other one ought to be so loved by all, nor can any other be so devoted to every one as he. Let every one together in him love one another so that by the love of one they may become one. That love is given to each one, yet it is not private; it is singular, yet not bereft of companionship; it is shared, yet remains whole; common to all, yet known fully by each of the elect; in sum it is the individual love of all and the complete love of each. Neither diminished by participation nor exhausted by use nor aged with time, it is at once old and new, desirable in its affection, sweet to experience, lasting forever, full of joy, refreshing, satisfying, and never a cause of satiety.

*His Soul:* What you say is very pleasing and I admit that I am now beginning more ardently to desire this love, whereas in the past I had disdained it too much. One thing remains now for explanation, and if I can learn this from you, I will not hesitate to say that I am satisfied in every regard. Is it in any way possible to explain how that most pure lover is present both in spirit and in reality to each of those whom he loves as he is to all of them? I shall not doubt his zeal, if I know that in fact he is truly present.

*Man:* My Soul, if you are so determined in this inquiry and cannot be satisfied unless you straightaway recognize the singularly valuable gift of your espoused, I gladly accede to your request. For I feel certain that your insistence stems more from devotion than from any importunate desire. In this matter also your most excellent lover has provided so that you would have something in which especially to rejoice. For just as he has granted common and special benefits, so has he also given personal ones. Common goods are those which all beings enjoy, such as the light of the sun or the breezes of the air. Again, special benefits are not given to all but to particular groups; examples of these are faith, wisdom, and education. Lastly, particular blessings are bestowed upon individual persons, examples of which are the primacy among the apostles to Peter, the apostolate of the gentiles to Paul, and the special privilege of love to John.

Now consider, my Soul, what gifts you have received to be held in common with all, what to be shared with some, and what to be specifically yours alone. In all his gifts he has revealed his love for you, whether in those which he has granted in common with everyone; or in those given especially to you and certain other persons; or in those particularly granted for yourself alone. Again, he has loved you with all those to whom he joined you in the sharing of his bounty. He has loved you before all those over whom you received preference in the gift of a particular grace. Among all the creatures of the universe you are his beloved, together with all good men you are dear to him, and more than all the wicked of this world you are his delight. And lest it seem slight to you to be preferred to all evil men, how many good are there who have received less than you? But I perceive that in your desire for a personal love you are quite concerned with individual goods, and although much up to now might have been said concerning those among whom and with whom you are loved, I think what has now been said on that point will suffice. I do not wish, however, that you make light of the effusion and excellence of the blessings with which you have been loved, since you have all good men for your companions and since the wicked and all things in the universe are subject to you. You have seen then, my Soul, the grandeur of his benefactions to you and the quality of those with whom you are loved.

Consider now, so far as you are able, the nature of your preferment. I tell you, my Soul, you know what you have received and it is now necessary to know more precisely, lest you begin to presume concerning things which you have not received or fail to give thanks for those you have. Would that I might treat these matters in a manner profitable to you and pleasing to him, the giver of these gifts. For he himself bestowed them upon you in order that you might always keep them in mind and never by forgetfulness grow cold in your love of him. First think on this, my Soul: there was once a time when you did not exist and in order that you might come into being, you received this as a gift from him. Thus existence was a gift of his. Now prior to your coming into being had you given anything to him which might be equal to this gift? Nothing, nothing whatever, since you were unable to give anything before you existed. In truth, your existence is a wholly gratuitous gift. To whom, therefore, have you been preferred by the fact of your existence? Is anyone able to receive less than this? And yet, unless something were there to receive existence, it would not be possible for the non-existent to begin. And unless existence were better than non-existence, the one who exists would have received nothing more than the one who does not.[6]

Why then, my God, have you created me, unless you wished me to exist rather than not to? Truly you have loved me more than all those who have not received this gift from you. In giving me existence, my God, you have given me a good and great, a good and excellent blessing, and I have received precedence over all those to whom you have not deigned to give this bounty. My Soul, what can we say when we speak to our God, to Him[7] who created us who were not and who have received more than all those who do not exist? Indeed, we say this and we say much in so speaking and we ought always to say this: Let us never forget Him from whom we have received so great a blessing. For if He had given nothing more, He would always have merited our praise and our love for this great gift. But He has given more for we have received not merely existence but a beautiful and fair existence. Just as our being surpasses nothingness through existence, so does it through its beauty of form surpass the indeterminate. And as existence is pleasing, so ordered existence is even more pleasing.[8] In this, my Soul, observe that you are preferred to all who have not received so excellent a gift of existence.

---

[6] The metaphysical principle of the goodness of being as such is applied, but not explicitly, in the philosophy of the Victorine.

[7] I have arbitrarily chosen this as the point at which to begin capitalizing pronominal references to God, because from here to the conclusion of the *Soliloquy* his identity as Lover and Benefactor is continually obvious to the second interlocutor, the Soul.

[8] The form here in question consists in the aspect of things, in the distribution of their parts. Hugh uses the term *informis* to designate a confused distribution and the term *formosus* to indicate an ordered arrangement of the parts of an object. cf. *De sacramentis*, 1, 1, 13; PL 176, 188-189. See Ledrus, "Hugues . . .," p. 33, concerning the spiritual correspondence of this subject: the soul has form in so far as it is enlightened, i.e., perceptive. The soul does not have order, properly speaking, because it is simple; but by reason it becomes the principle of order.

But the bounty of the Divine Bestower could not be stayed here. He has given us something more, for He has raised us to the level of his own likeness. As He took us to himself in his love, so He also wished to make us like himself. Therefore, having granted both existence and harmony to us, He also gave us life of such a type that by its essence we might excel what does not exist, by its beauty what is disordered, and by its mode of life what is inanimate. You are under a great obligation, my Soul, for you have received much and of yourself you have nothing. You have nothing whatever to give in return for all these things, except only your love. For what has been given you in love cannot be requited more fittingly and properly than by your love. And you have received all this in love. God could have given life to many others, but you were the object of his great love by this gift. Yet He did not love you more because he found you to be more worthy of his love. Rather, because He freely loved you in this manner, He made you such that He now loves you as one truly worthy of his devotion.

*His Soul:* The more I hear, the more I wish to hear. Go on, I beg of you, and tell me what follows.

*Man:* After existence, beauty, and life, the senses and intelligence were given to you with the same divine love. For without this love the Giver would not have granted anything nor the receiver obtained anything. How exalted and glorious you have been made, my Soul! What does such attire signify but that He who clothed you has been preparing you as his spouse for his bridal chamber? He knew for what sweet task you were destined and what raiment was needed; therefore, He gave what was fitting. And so well did it become you that He Himself delighted in these very gifts.

Without He adorned you with the senses, within He enlightened you with wisdom, giving the one as an outer garment, the other as inner garb. His gifts of the senses are, as it were, precious and resplendent jewels for display, and the faculty of wisdom within is like the natural beauty of your countenance. Indeed, your attire far surpasses the beauty of any gems and your countenance is the most beautiful of all. Certainly such beauty is most befitting for one who would enter into the chamber of our Heavenly King. Oh, how greatly have you been loved and to how many have you been preferred in being honored in this manner. What a singular gift was given you, one not granted to all but only to those who are loved and are worthy to be loved by Him. You had much to rejoice in and you ought to have guarded your treasure closely in order not to destroy or defile this incomparable gift, nor to disfigure such great beauty. Had it been lost or unguarded you would have become more miserable than if in utter abjectness you had never received this gift and had never known its perfection. If the disorder of corruption punished you with the loss of this great blessing, in your fall you would have become more vile than if you had never known this gift. Therefore, it should have been guarded and protected so that it might continue in your custody and its loss never come to pass.

Yet, consider what you have done, my Soul. You have deserted your Lover and have squandered your affections on others. You have lost your probity, defiled your beauty, wasted your substance. You have become cheap, debased, and impure, hardly worthy any longer of the embraces of your Lover. You have forgotten your Espoused and have failed to respond rightly to His great generosity. You have become as a harlot; from the excesses of debauchery your breasts have become slack, your brow wrinkled, your cheeks faded, your eyes dull and clouded, your lips pallid, and your flesh withered. You have dissipated your strength and even to your lovers you are now hateful.[9]

*His Soul:* I was hoping that such great praise would lead to a different conclusion, but I see now that you have spoken these words for my discomfiture and to show me to be worthy rather of disdain. Since I accepted but did not preserve these benefactions you have proven me to be an utter ingrate. I wish that all this had not come about, or at least that you had not mentioned it, so that oblivion might cover my embarrassment, even if my pride has not avoided its fall.[10]

*Man:* These words were spoken to enlighten you, not to confuse.[11] I desired to make you more vividly aware of your obligations to Him who created you from nothingness and redeemed you from damnation. I made mention of these matters to give proof of His love, and they now will give me the opportunity to tell how much your Lover, who appeared so sublime when He created you, permitted himself to be humbled when

---

[9] These expressions and comparisons are inspired by the warnings of God to his people in *Ezechiel.* They are not too strong to convey the horror of infidelity which the spirit experiences after it begins to sense God's goodness and love.

[10] The *Soliloquy* has produced its desired immediate effect: contempt of self or contrition, "the sense of sorrow which touches the heart when it considers its failings." (*De modo orandi*, 1; PL 176, 979.) From this sorrow, in the light of the divine mercy, comes "the turning toward God, the sentiment of genuine and pious affection" which is called devotion, and "which prayer makes perfect." (Ib.) "What can better stir man to a desire to pray than his misery and distress in the evils which overwhelm him, and what is more attractive than the mercy of his Creator, experienced so often in the midst of these evils." (Ib. 977.)

[11] "So far as a soul is in the state of sin it is in darkness and confusion. It cannot escape this confusion and put things in order according to justice and truth unless it has been previously enlightened concerning its failings to see the light in the darkness, that is to say, the good in the bad; this in order to discipline itself and conform to the truth. The soul which is in confusion cannot do this without light. That is why light must first be cast, so that the soul can see itself and recognize the horror and misery of its condition, so that it can despise itself and dispose itself according to the truth. When all has been set aright and disposed according to reason and wisdom, then will suddenly shine the sun of justice, according to the promise: Blessed are the pure in heart for they shall see God." (*De sacramentis*, 1, 1, 12; PL 176, 195.)

[25]

He redeemed you. Then He was exalted, now He is brought low; yet now as then He is ever lovable because He is ever admirable. Then He did wondrous things to you in His great power; now in His mercy He has submitted Himself to the punishment in your stead. That He might return you to the high station from which you fell He deigned to come down to you in your degradation, and to redeem for you in justice what you had wasted away, in His compassion He permitted Himself to suffer the penalties which were yours. Therefore did He descend, take up the burden, suffer under it, overcome it, and redeem the debt. In fine, He came down among men, took on their mortality, suffered His passion, conquered death, and restored mankind.

My Soul, do you not grow dumb in the face of such wonders and such blessings given for your sake? Consider how much He loves you who willed to do so much in your behalf. By His grace you had been made beautiful, but you were defiled through your own wickedness. Yet again you have been purified and made whole by His devotion; here as before His mercy has been seen. When you were not, His great love brought you into being, and when you became degraded, He remained devoted to you in order to restore your beauty and reveal to you how greatly He desired you. He even willed to free you from your fate by dying on your behalf, so that He made plain not only the blessings of His devotion but also the zeal of His charity. Indeed He now loves you with true charity, just as if you had always remained close to Him. There is neither reproach for your failings nor arrogance in His benefactions. If then you should wish for the future to persevere with Him, to love Him as is fitting, and to keep without blemish your heart for Him, He promises you blessings even greater than before.

*His Soul:* Now in a certain manner I am beginning to like my failings because, as I see, it was no small advantage to have done wrong. For through them it has been revealed to me as clear as the day what I was desiring to know with all my heart. O happy fault! While He in His charity is drawn to me to remove that fault, this same charity is revealed to my desire and the burning aspirations of my heart. I would never have recognized His love so clearly if I had not experienced it in such great dangers. How fortunate I was to fall, for I have risen up the happier. There is no greater affection, no more true love, no more blessed charity, no more ardent desire than His. In His innocence He died for me, in whom there was certainly nothing to love. Why then, O Lord, have You loved me and so greatly loved me that You should die for me? What of worth did You see in me for which You could will to endure such sufferings?

*Man:* My Soul, accuse yourself before your Lord, because until this very day you were unthankful for His great blessings and unwilling to

[26]

acknowledge His many mercies. But in order that you may better recognize all that you owe Him, listen closely while I set forth in order His other benefactions to you.

*His Soul:* I am so desirous to hear what is sweet to me that I would have you repeat incessantly what has now been said if I were not anxious to hear what remains to be said.

*Man:* Well then, you had fallen away and were lost, and because you were in bondage to your sins[12] He came in order to redeem you. So great was His love that He gave His own blood as the price of your recovery. Such was the manner by which He brought you out of exile and redeemed you from bondage.

*His Soul:* I was utterly ignorant of the great love my God had for me. I must not be base in my own eyes if I was so pleasing to God that He chose to die in my stead in order not to lose me.

*Man:* What if you began to consider the vast numbers and types of men who have been rejected, who could not receive the favor which has been given you! Certainly you have heard of the many generations of men from the beginning of time to the present, who, deprived of the knowledge of God and the price of their redemption, have fallen into eternal damnation. Your Redeemer and Lover has preferred you to all these men by the gift of His grace, which none of these merited to receive. What will you say? Why do you think you have been favored over these? Is it because you were stronger, wiser, more noble, or wealthier than all these that you merited to receive this special favor in preference to them all? How many valiant, wise, noble, and wealthy men lived in that span? Yet all of them were abandoned and left to perish! You alone have been accepted before all these, and if you should seek the cause for this you would find no other reason than the free and gratuitous charity of your Savior. He as your Espoused, your Lover, your Redeemer, and your God selected and foredestined you. He chose you from among all these, He took you up from them, and He loved you in preference to them all. In His own name He called you that you might always remember it. He desired you to partake of that name, to share in the truth of that name. He anointed you with the unction of gladness, with which He Himself had been anointed. Thus he who by Christ is called a Christian has been anointed with this unction.[13]

---

[12] See St. Paul, *Romans* 7, 14.

[13] The Greek etymology: *chrio*—I anoint; *chrisma, christos;* intrigues the writer. "The anointing with chrism was established in antiquity, as we read in the Old Testament; in those times only kings and priests were anointed. This prefigured the Anointed *par excellence*, Him with whom we share both this blessing and His name. 'Christ' in effect derives from *chrisma* (chrism), and 'Christian' from 'Christ'. This is why all those to whom the name of Christ has been given ought to receive His unction, for in Christ we are a chosen people, a royal priesthood. The chrism consists of oil and balm; the oil signifies the infusion of grace, and the balm the fragrance of a good name." (*De sacramentis*, 2, 7, 1; *PL* 176, 459.)

*His Soul:* I confess that I have received much, but I ask you one question. If, as you say, I have been selected as His very own, why the delay? Why have I never yet known the embraces of my Beloved?

*Man:* You are truly in ignorance, my Soul. You do not know how vile you have been in the past, how degraded, how ugly and filthy, unkempt, and dissipated. You were certainly loathsome and unclean. How can you therefore seek to go so quickly into that chamber of modesty and chasteness, unless by some care and zeal you first regain your former comeliness? This is the reason for the delay, this is why your Beloved has withdrawn from you and has neither embraced you nor given His sweet kisses to you. For truly the defiled ought not to touch the clean nor should a base person have sight of the beautiful. However, when you have been fittingly prepared and clothed, without embarrassment you will at last enter into and remain in the bridal chamber of your heavenly Spouse. Then your past disgrace will be no source of shame to you, for you will be free of all stain and reproach. Therefore be zealous to prepare yourself: to beautify your face, to set aright your garments, to wipe away all stains, to become clean again, to change your habits, to keep to the right, and with all your ways changed for the better to present yourself finally as a worthy lover of a most excellent Spouse.

Now I also wish to give some advice in order to make you more cautious. For since you have heard of your preferment it is possible that either high spirits will make you arrogant or neglect of your duties make you lax. Have you ever heard the story of what King Assuerus[14] did when he dismissed Vashti, the queen, because of her insolence? It tells of a remarkable tale, a useful example, and a serious danger.[15] This woman was sent away because of her pride. An order went forth from the king that from all the ends of his kingdom the most beautiful young virgins be brought to the city of Susa and there be placed in a sanctuary under the care of the eunuch Egeus, who was the overseer and guardian of the royal women. There they would receive clean garments and other items necessary for their use. Because of the king's desire to please, they would be fitted out and adorned with every necessity. For six months they would be anointed with oil of myrtle, and for another six they would make use of certain cosmetics. Thus prepared and adorned they would

---

14 "Assuerus, a rich and powerful king, is a type for Christ, by the significance of his name, the prestige of his position, and the grandeur of his wealth. By the meaning of his name, for it signifies 'door', and Christ has said: I am the door. (*John* 10, 7); by the prestige of his power, for all power in heaven and on earth has been given to Christ. (*Mat.* 28, 18); and by the grandeur of his riches, for all that the Father possesses has been given to the Son. (*John* 17, 10)." (*Allegoriae in vetus testamentum*, 9, 1; *PL* 175, 733).

15 The writer here uses the practice of the *lectio* in order to rise to a description of ecstasy. The reading includes history, allegory, and tropology. The history, which begins at this point, consists in narrating what occurred. (*De sacramentis*, Prologus, 4; *PL* 176, 184). The text is from *Esther* 2, 1-4.

pass from their sanctuary into the chamber of the king and the one who was most pleasing in the eyes of the king would take the place of Vashti upon the royal throne. Consider how many were chosen that one alone might be selected, the one who of all seemed the most beautiful and the best adorned in the eyes of the king. The ministers of the king might choose many for this course of preparation, but the king could select only one for his bedchamber. The first choosing of the many was accomplished by the order of the king, but the final selection of the one by the will of the king. Let us consider, therefore, if this example can be adapted to the matter which concerns us here.[16]

A King, the son of the greatest King, came into this world,[17] which He Himself had created, to seek a consort for Himself, who would be a chosen and peerless spouse and one worthy of the royal nuptials. But because Judaea despised and rejected Him as He appeared in the garb of humility, she was herself rejected. And so ministers of the King were sent forth as apostles to bring together souls throughout the world and lead them to the city of the King, which is His holy Church. Therein is the home and palace of the royal consorts, that is, of holy souls who are made fruitful and bring forth offspring not for servitude but for the kingdom. Because they serve God in charity and not in fear, they bring forth their own for the liberty of good works.[18] Many are the called, then, who enter the Church through faith and who receive there the sacraments of Christ. These are like certain unguents and specifics prepared for the regeneration and beautification of souls. But because it is truly said that "Many are called but few are chosen," not all who are received into this regimen will be selected for the kingdom, but only those who are zealous to cleanse and prepare themselves by these means, that when they are brought into the presence of the King they may be found such as He Himself would select and not cast away.[19]

Look, therefore, where you are and you will realize what you ought to do. Your Spouse brought you to the couch where the candidates are

---

[16] Here history gives way to allegory, which seeks to find in the story another reality, present, past, or future. (*De sacramentis*, Prologus 4; *PL* 176, 184; cf. *Didascalion*, 6, 4; *PL* 176, 802.)

[17] Hugh presents the symbol of Christ the King in diverse ways. The following allegory reminds us that the writer lived in the time of the Crusades: "The Word Incarnate is our King who comes into this world to fight the Devil. All the saints who lived before His coming march as soldiers before their King; all those who lived after Him and will live even to the end of time are soldiers who follow their King. He advances in the midst of His army, escorted and protected by His troops. And though one sees the arms of many nations in so large a multitude, the sacraments and rituals of all who precede and follow, all are nevertheless devoted to fight only for this King, to follow only His standard, to search out this enemy, and to gain the crown of this victory." (*De sacramentis*, Prologus 2; *PL* 176, 183).

[18] Cf. St. Paul, *Gal.* 4, 21-31.

[19] At this point the tropology is introduced, which describes in the story what one ought to do. (*De sacramentis*, Prologus 4; *PL* 176, 185).

prepared. He gave you various cosmetics and preparations, and ordered that various delicacies from the royal table be given you. Whatever benefits your health or recovery, whatever can bring back or increase your beauty has been readied for you. Take care, then, lest you neglect to prepare yourself, lest when at last you are brought into His presence you be found unworthy, God forbid, of His company. Prepare yourself as is needful for a spouse of a King, a spouse of the King of Heaven, a spouse of the immortal Lover.

*His Soul:* Once again you have filled me with bitterness and have stricken me with not a little fear. If I understand your words correctly, I am now changed in disposition, but have not avoided the danger. I am indeed changed, because from that vague and uncertain infatuation which once plagued me I have turned to the one, true Love. Yet I have not averted the danger because as you say, unless I show myself worthy in every way, I will not achieve the realization of this love. Therefore it now remains for you to instruct me in earnest about this regimen by which the royal consorts are prepared, about the royal diet given them, the ointments with which they are bathed and all other matters concerning this preparation and treatment. His love inflames me and so I desire to acquire all those arts without which I cannot gain His affection. Oh that I might merit to be that one whose beauty and grace the King will praise! How happy that one will be, the elected of the elect, whose zeal will gain the goal. How slight I shall think the effort to be, if I can thereby bring my hopes to this end. So I beg you not to be unwilling to teach me those particular remedies by which I must renew my features for this trial. For I greatly desire to please Him, whose charity to me I see is so benign and whose love so sweet.

*Man:* You must do as follows, and I pray that He who gave you the will to do this much will also grant you the strength to see it through. You ask me what this sanctum of preparation is and what the chamber of the King? Give thought to those two places for it is necessary that you consider them. In the former the espoused are prepared for the nuptials and in the latter the bonds are consummated. The Church is like the room of preparation, in which the spouses of God are now made ready for their future nuptials, and the heavenly Jerusalem is like the chamber of the King in which the rites are completed. After the time of preparation in their quarters they pass into the compartment of the King, because after a time of good works they come to obtain the fruit of these works. The earthly Church is truly called a place of preparation because of the three orders of the faithful, married persons and celibates, both those who serve the Church and those who live in the world.

Let us consider next the kinds of ointments and cosmetics, the diet, and the vestments which are made ready in the regimen of the espoused.

Nor should this be passed over because just as their Spouse from the first freely loved these souls who were defiled and base in some manner or other, so does He also freely give them every means for their rehabilitation. Of themselves they possess nothing by which they can please Him, for they have received everything from Him. Hence if you have anything with which to adorn yourself, realize that it is evidence of His love. You have nothing which does not come from Him.

In this room of preparation you will first find the font of baptism and the basin of regeneration in which you wash away the stain of past sins. Next the chrism and the oil, in the unction of which you are bathed by the Holy Spirit. Then anointed and imbued with the unction of gladness you come to the table and take there the nourishment of the body and blood of Christ. Filled and refreshed within by this you dispel the harmful emaciation of previous hungers and in a wondrous manner are rejuvenated with the recovery of your former strength and figure. Next you put on the garments of good works and by the fruit of almsgiving, with fasts and prayers, with holy vigils and other deeds of piety you become arrayed as though with finery of the most varied kinds. Finally the fragrance of the virtues comes forth and their sweet odors welling up dispel all the stench of past filth, so that somehow you seem to be wholly changed and to be transformed into someone else. You are become more joyful, more keen, more vigorous. The mirror that is Holy Scripture is also given to you so that you may see there your own visage and know that the arrangement of your garments does not have anything unfitting.

What, therefore, do you say, my Soul? Do you know whether you have yet perceived any of these things? Certainly you were washed clean in the font and also received the anointing with the chrism; certainly you ate and drank the same nourishment at the table of the King. But it may be that you were again defiled. If so, your tears can wash you clean again. If the effects of the anointing have been lost on you, by good and pious devotion you can anoint yourself again. If you are consumed by daily hunger, cleansed by your tears and refreshed by the unction of true contrition you can again regain your strength.

See how on every side you are aided by the divine plan! You had not and you received; you wasted your substance and it is restored to you. You will never be utterly abandoned and thus you know how greatly you are esteemed by your Lover. He does not want to lose you, and so with the greatest patience He awaits and restores you, if you ask it, you so often lost through your own fault. How many have perished who once with you had accepted these gifts, but who did not merit to receive them back again with you after losing them. You, therefore, have been loved more than all those, because what was lost has been graciously returned to you, while this has been strictly denied to them. Has no grace of doing good works been given you? A good will as the gift of your Lover has not been withheld. If you do great things, by His mercy are you raised up, and if you do not, perhaps you are humbled for your good. It may be that you do not have the grace of the virtues, but then the assaults of the vices strengthen you in humility. More sweet is the odor of true humility to God than that of virtue which is puffed up. Guard always against hastiness in judging his Providence, but beg Him always with fear and reverence to help you as He knows best. Pray that in His mercy He will cleanse you if any sins now remain in you, that in His benignity He will perfect whatever spark of virtue you may possess, and that He will bring you to Himself in the way He has ordained. What more can I say to you? Is there anything further we can say to make clear His devotion? I ask you, my Soul, is there anything to add? What do you say? If you speak of what pertains to yourself, you will not mention the concerns of others; and if of others and yourself, yet not everything that could be said. For who can discuss all that might be said? And yet we know that the source of all things is charity.

Consider two men, both noble and both born in the same hour. The one is left in poverty, the other is exalted by wealth, yet charity works in both, for to the one it gives humility in his poverty, and to the other consolation in his abundance. This man is weak and that one strong, but the latter is restrained lest he work evil and the former is strengthened so that he may grow vigorous in good works. Charity makes trial of each one; it does not condemn. The one is enlightened by wisdom, the other is left with the simplicity of his own good sense; this one that he may be eager to despise himself, that one that he may recognize his Creator; yet to each is charity present. Such is the love of God for us, that everything which our human frailty endures is disposed in His great benevolence for our welfare.

### CONFESSION

I confess to You your mercies, my Lord and my God, because You have not deserted me, O Sweetness of my life and Light of my eyes. What shall I return to You for all You have given me?[20] You wish me to love You; yet how shall I love You and how greatly shall I love You? Who am I that I should love You? And yet I shall, my Lord and my Strength, my Support, my Refuge, my Liberator, my God, my Helper, my Protector, the Pledge of my Salvation, and my Surety.[21] What more can I say?

---

[20] *Ps.* 115, 3 (*Vulg.*)
[21] *Ps.* 17, 2-3 (*Vulg.*) Prayer has suddenly succeeded meditation, and it is prayer in its more perfect form according to Hugh. "Pure prayer occurs when the soul is so inflamed with devotion that, after turning to God to request some favor, it forgets in the intensity of its love the object of its request; desirous of enjoying this love, eager to devote itself freely to it, the soul leaves at once the cares which brought it to begin the prayer." (*De modo orandi.* 2; PL 176, 980).

You are my Lord and my God. My Soul, what shall we do for our Lord God, from whom we have received so many great blessings? He certainly was not satisfied to grant us the same goods which He gave to others. Even in our trials and misdeeds we have recognized Him as our particular Lover, and so we should love Him utterly, in good times and bad. You have so endowed me, O Lord, to recognize You and understand better than many others the revelations of your secrets. You have left my contemporaries in the darkness of ignorance, but in me You have infused the light of wisdom. You have granted that I know You more truly, love You more purely, believe in You more surely, and pursue You more ardently. You have given me many gifts: keen senses, an able intellect, good memory, fluent speech, a pleasing manner of discourse, ability to persuade, talent in my work, a pleasant personality in discussion, progress in studies, success in my enterprises, comfort in adversity, and wisdom in prosperity. Wherever I have applied myself, there Your favor and mercy have preceded me. Often when I seemed about to falter, You suddenly came to my help. When I was lost, You led me back to the way; when I was in ignorance, You taught me; when I sinned, You took me up. In sadness You consoled me, in despair You comforted me. If I fell, You raised me up; if I stood erect, You sustained me. All these and many other things You have done for me, O Lord. It will be sweet always to think of them, always to speak of them, ever to give thanks for them. In this way I shall praise You and love You, O Lord God, for all Your blessings.[22] Behold, my Soul, you have your earnest money and because of it you can recognize your Spouse. Keep yourself untouched, undefiled, pure, and without stain for Him. If once you were a harlot, now you have become a virgin, for His love has been pleased to give back to sinners their spotlessness and to preserve for the innocent their chastity. Never forget, therefore, how much mercy He has shown you and how greatly you are loved by Him, for you know that His blessing has never failed you.

*His Soul:* Truly I confess that His love is worthily called singular, for although it bestows itself upon many, it embraces each one individually. It is certainly a good and wonderful blessing, for it is the common possession of all and the complete delight of each one. It watches over all and fulfills the desires of each one; it is everywhere present, takes care of everyone, and yet is equally provident for the individual. When I consider His mercies all around me it seems certain that in some way (if it is right to speak in this manner) God does nothing except provide for my

---

[22] Hugh describes here a manner of prayer which simply and intuitively perceives the action of divine goodness. This is an attitude of faith which makes the soul keenly aware that all is in the hands of God. In his intensity the writer describes these feelings and perceptions as if they were the result of a wholly natural process.

welfare. I see Him wholly devoted to my care, as if He were forgetful of everyone else and wished to have time for me alone. He is always present, always ready. Whithersoever I turn, He does not desert me; whereever I am, He is with me; whatever I do, He helps me. In sum, He makes plain by the effect of His aid that He is the ever-present overseer of all my thoughts and actions, and that He is my personal co-worker in everything that requires His assistance.

Hence it must be admitted that if His countenance cannot be seen by us, His presence can never be escaped. Because of this I confess that after seriously considering the matter I am confounded by fear and great shame; for I see now that He, whom I so greatly desire to please, is everywhere with me and is an observer of my most hidden thoughts and acts. How many are the faults for which I blush in His sight and on account of which I am greatly fearful of offending Him. And how few are those characteristics in me worthy of praise (are there any?), in which I trust He will be pleased. Would that I might hide from His sight for a while, until I wipe away those stains and then come before Him immaculate and free from blemish; for how can I please Him in my present degradation, which is even revolting to me? O stains of long standing, O stains that disfigure and dishonor, how much longer will you remain? Go! Depart, and offend no longer the eyes of my Beloved. Be not deceived, for you will not remain with me once His help is given, even though in my sloth I have thus far been unable to remove you. I have sworn not to keep or desire you any longer, for I utterly loath and detest your baseness. And so, even if I could not be seen by my Espoused, I would not wish to be polluted by you: but for more than this I reject you because I am visible to Him and any rebuff to Him saddens me more than does my own turpitude. Therefore depart, for in vain will you cling to me further. Even if you remain, you will not be mine for I consider you as strangers to me and I shall have nothing more to do with you. I now have another Exemplar to whom I wish to conform and to whom I unceasingly look. So far as I can, I desire to become more and more like Him. From Him I have learned that I ought to remove you, and now I know how I shall do this.

*Man:* Something wonderful is happening to us, but perhaps you are not amazed because you do not perceive what I want to say. I am thinking of how from the beginning of our talk you brought forward points which seemed to deny that love. By these arguments the strength of this love has never been undermined; instead it has been more fully confirmed. You said, for example, that an individual love and one held in common with others were mutually impossible. But then that love has been shown to be more truly marvelous because it is at once held in common by many and yet in an especial way bestowed on each one.

Again, you said that you were not perfectly loved because you had heard that you were chosen for His regimen of preparation, but you had not yet seen yourself taken to His chambers; yet here too His love for you has been revealed to be even greater because your self-reform is patiently awaited by Him.

Finally, you began to doubt whether in your shameful condition you could be loved by Him, even though you unwillingly suffered this ugliness. Yet do you not remember that once you were completely loathsome and were beloved by Him? If, therefore, He deigned to love you when you were wholly repulsive and possessed no attraction, how much more does He now desire you, now that you are beginning to be beautiful and to put aside your former vileness. For the fact that He considered you in your imperfections worthy of His love also redounds to His praise. And although He sees certain qualities in you which do not please Him, He is yet glad that you have also begun to loathe these faults which He dislikes. He does not consider your present condition so much as your prospects, nor what you are, but what you wish to be, and only that you do your utmost to become such as you have thus far failed to become.

*His Soul:* I now ask that you kindly answer this last question. What is that sweetness which sometimes touches my consciousness, and so forcefully and pleasantly moves me that I begin somehow to be wholly changed and in some way to be transported? Suddenly I am renewed and am become totally different, and I experience a well-being beyond my ability to describe. My senses are exhilarated, all the misery of past sorrows falls away, my mind is exultant, and my perception enlightened. My heart also is cheered and my desires are pleased. Now I see myself in some other place, I know not where, and as it were I hold someone within me in the embraces of love. Who it is I do not know, and yet I struggle with great effort to retain Him in my possession and never lose Him. My mind somehow fights in a pleasureable way lest He ever depart, for it desires to be always in His embrace. And as if it would find in Him the fulfillment of all its desires, it hopes for nothing more, seeks nothing beyond, wishes always to be like this, completely and ineffably rejoicing. Is that one my Beloved? Say, I ask you, that I may know whether He is that one; then if He should come to me again, I will beseech Him not to depart, but to remain forever.

*Man:* Certainly that one who comes to you is your Beloved. But He comes hidden, unseen, and imperceptible. He comes to touch you, not to be seen by you; to admonish you, not to be beheld. He comes not to give Himself entirely, but to present Himself to your awareness; not to fulfill your desires, but to gain your affection. He offers the first and certain signs of His love, not the plenitude of its perfect fulfillment! In this especially is there evidence of the pledge of your espousal, for He who in the future will permit Himself to be contemplated and possessed by you forever now presents Himself to you that you may know how well-disposed He is. Meanwhile you are consoled in His absence, since by His visits you are continually refreshed lest you grow weak. My Soul, we have now said many things; but after all these words I ask you to acknowledge Him only, love Him only, pursue Him only, take Him only, and possess Him only.

*His Soul:*   This is my wish and my desire, and I seek this with all my heart.

# Bibliography

Copleston, F. *A History of Philosophy* II: *Mediaeval Philosophy, Augustine to Scotus* (Burns, Oates, & Washbourne: London, 1950)

De Wulf, M. *History of Mediaeval Philosophy* I (Longmans, Green and Company: London, 1926)

Geyer, B. *Die patristische und scholastische Zeit* in F. Ueberweg *Grundriss der Geschichte der Philosophie,* Part 2 (E. S. Mittler: Berlin, 1928) 261-269; 709.

Gilson, E. *La philosophie au moyen âge,* 2éd. (Payot: Paris, 1944)

——————— *History of Christian Philosophy in the Middle Ages* (Random House: New York, 1955)

Haureau, B. *Hugues de St. Victor: Nouvel examen d'édition de ses oeuvres* (Pagneere: Paris, 1859)

——————— *Les oeuvres de Hugues de St. Victor, essai critique* (Hatchette: Paris, 1886)

Ledrus, M. "Hugues de St. Victor: Le gage des divine fiançailles *(De arrha animae),*" *Museum Lessianum, Compagnie de Jesus, Section ascetique et mystique,* 12 (Louvain, 1923)

Migne, J. P. *Patrologiae Cursus, series Latina* CLXXV-CLXXVII (Garnier: Paris, 1879)

Müller, K. "Hugo von St. Victor: *Soliloquium de arrha animae* und *De vanitate mundi,*" *Kleine Texte für Vorlesungen und Uebungen,* H. Lietzmann (ed.) No. 123 (Bonn, 1913)

——————— "Zur Mystik Hugos von St. Victor," *Zeitschrift für Kirchengeschichte* 45 (1926) 175-189.

Myers, Edw. "Hugh of St. Victor," *The Catholic Encyclopedia* VII (Robert Appleton Company: New York, 1910); see Index Vol. XVI, 927, for related topics on mysticism and mystical theology.

Ostler, H. "Die Psychologie des Hugo von St. Viktor," *Beiträge zur Geschichte der Philosophie des Mittelalters* 6, 1 (Aschendorff: Münster i. W., 1906)

Pittenger, W. "The Incarnational Philosophy of Hugh of St. Victor," *Theology* 31 (1935) 274-278.

Rousselot, P. "Pour l'histoire du probleme de l'amour au moyen âge," *Beiträge zur Geschichte der Philosophie des Mittelalters* 6, 6 (Aschendorff: Münster i. W., 1908)

Vernet, F. "Hugues de St. Victor," *Dictionnaire de theologie catholique* VII (Letouzey et Ané: Paris, 1927) 240-308.

——————— *Medieval Spirituality* (Sands & Co.: London, 1930)